MW00413179

THE POST PANDEMIC
PRAYER GUIDE

Start a Prayer Revolution

BISHOP EDWARD PEECHER

URIEL PRESS

Copyright © 2023 by Bishop Edward Peecher
All rights reserved.

No part of this book may be reproduced in any form or by any means, electronic or mechanical, including photocopying, recording, video, or by any information or retrieval system, without prior written permission from the publisher except for the use of brief quotations in a book review.

Scripture quotations are from the New King James Version Bible, English Standard Version Bible, and New International Version Bible.

Published in the United States by Uriel Press
P.O. Box 436987, Chicago, IL 60643
www.urielpress.com

ISBN 978-0-9601047-7-2 (paperback)
ISBN 978-0-9601047-8-9 (eBook)

Cover design by Laura Duffy

Printed in the United States of America

Get The Post Pandemic Prayer Guide app and expand your prayer life.

Scan the QR code below to get access:

TABLE OF CONTENTS

Preface vii

**PART ONE: UNDERSTANDING THE
            SCRIPTURE** 1

Chapter 1: "When you pray, say…" (Luke 11:2) 3

Chapter 2: "Our Father in Heaven" 10

Chapter 3: "Your Kingdom Come, Your Will Be
            Done on Earth As It Is in Heaven". . . . 15

Chapter 4: "Give Us This Day Our Daily Bread" . . 25

Chapter 5: "Forgive Us Our Debts as We Forgive
            Our Debtors". 30

Chapter 6: "Deliver Us From the Evil One" 36

PART TWO: STRATEGICALLY PRAYING THE PRAYER **47**

Chapter 7: Personal Benefit. 49

Chapter 8: Start a Movement of Healing for the Nation. 53

About Bishop Edward Peecher 58

PREFACE

This little prayer manual came to me as I struggled to keep my spiritual walk fresh during the seemingly endless months of the quarantine brought on by the Covid-19 global pandemic. Up until that point in my life, I had maintained a consistent prayer and devotional life since I gave my heart to Christ in 1973. I enrolled in Moody Bible Institute in 1974 and preached my first sermon in that year also.

I was a full-time pastor from 1985 to 2016, and I have preached countless sermons on prayer. Yet here I was in 2021, struggling to keep my own prayer life and spiritual life fresh. As I persevered, the Lord began to reveal this simple lesson that I am about to share with you.

This little book is addressed to you, all my brothers and sisters, who wake up every morning hoping with all your heart that today you will have a closer and more fulfilling walk with Christ, but by the end of most days, you feel like you haven't moved the needle much. I feel you.

You are not alone in your pursuit, and your future is far brighter than your present circumstances seem to suggest. This little book is going to help you.

This book is also directed to congregational and denominational leaders. It can be a tool to motivate and mobilize the members of your flock, be it local, regional, or national, to adopt a common vision and purpose and help them shine in the midst of these extraordinary times. Our nation desperately needs a healing balm.

Understand this: these times have not fallen on us— instead, we were chosen before the foundation of the world, and uniquely designed with our temperament and intelligence and perspective and placed in these times to be a part of a movement that will change the whole world around us.

This is not just a prayer manual; it is so much more. This is a tool that God will use to spark a prayer movement the likes of which the world has not seen. I urge you, along with this book, to scan the QR Code and download the "Post Pandemic Prayer Mobile App," and set the hours you want it to chime. Then on the hours you have selected, take forty-five seconds to remind yourself that you are part of God's kingdom by praying

"The Lord's Prayer," also known as "The Our Father," the prayer Jesus gave us to pray along with thousands of your brothers and sisters. Also visit our Facebook (@ TKTK) and Instagram (@TKTKT) accounts and post photos and comments to encourage your church family to become a part of this movement.

So I invite you to take this journey with me to revive your prayer life and awaken the world.

PART ONE

Understanding
The Scripture

CHAPTER 1

"WHEN YOU PRAY, SAY..."
(LUKE 11:2)

I was in the shower one morning, feeling dry in my soul and estranged from God. This was not a feeling that I was used to since I first began to walk with Christ. I gave my heart to Christ on November 13, 1973. Two months later, I enrolled in evening classes at Moody Bible Institute in Chicago. I preached my first sermon four months after enrolling in Bible school. I led my mother and father to faith in Christ, as well as my brother and three sisters. Eventually, my wife, Katie, came to faith in Christ. I led all three of my children to faith in Christ.

Within a year, I was on the preaching team at my home church, Grove Heights Conservative Baptist

Church, as an elder in training. I was passionate about my faith and shared it often.

Standing there in the shower with the warm water streaming down my face, I thought it had been way too long since my last real conversation with God and way too long since I had read more than just a few verses in my Bible. So, right there, in the shower, I was attempting to open up a little dialogue with God. Not out of a sense of obligation, this was just a desire to reconnect with my friend whom I loved, who I know loves me so much, a friend who I had neglected for several weeks.

As much as I have preached on prayer over the years, praying shouldn't have been a struggle for me right then, but it was. When I first started preaching back in 1974, I was young in the faith and fresh to the Bible. Everything was new and exciting. I was discovering new things in the Word of God almost every day, from my personal study and from my professors at Moody Bible Institute. As time progressed, I developed an approach to preaching. My goal was to find the truth in scriptures, first for my personal life, and then to share with others. While crafting a sermon message, my main two goals were to answer (1) what is the truth of the passage in focus, and (2) what does the application of that truth look like in everyday life?

I had also developed an approach to prayer, whether in the shower, or in my study, or walking down the street. That approach is guided by the prayer Jesus gave to the disciples in Matt. 6, commonly known as "The Lord's Prayer."

My understanding of that prayer is it is a guide or a format for prayer. My first encounter with that prayer was in my Catholic school upbringing. As a lad growing up in the Ida B. Wells housing projects on Chicago's south side in the 1950s, my siblings and I (seven of us altogether) attended Holy Angel's Catholic School. I learned the "Our Father" and the "Hail Mary" when I was eight years old.

As an altar boy, I owned a Rosary, and after our routine confessions, I would get assigned as an act of penance to pray three "Our Fathers" and nine "Hail Marys," which I prayed personally to God. For the first twenty-three years of my life, the "Our Father" and the "Hail Mary" were the only ways I knew how to pray.

Finally, it became too difficult for our parents to keep so many kids in Catholic school, so in 1963 they pulled us all out, and I finished eighth grade in Chicago public schools. Having left the Catholic school, I left all spiritual instruction. I went on to attend and graduate from Englewood High School.

As a trained minister, it was supposed to be easy for me to bring up words and expressions of adoration of

God's character and His glory, words of dedication to his Kingdom, and petitions of God's provision and protection from His enemy. But standing there under the stream of warm water from the showerhead, no words of adoration flowed up from my belly, no words of dedication or even words of petition came out of my heart. I just remembered the words of Jesus in Luke 11 saying: "When you pray, say: Our Father in Heaven, hallowed be your name. Your kingdom come, Your will be done, on Earth, as it is in heaven. Give us day by day our daily bread. And forgive us our sins, as we also forgive everyone who is indebted to us. And do not lead us into temptation, but deliver us from the evil one." (NKJV)

As I uttered those words out loud, many thoughts and ideas rushed into my mind. The power of those words given to us by Jesus Himself came alive inside me. The Word of God is life-giving, and it was giving life and sustenance to my dry soul. I was beginning to perk up. Then the thought started to occur to me, how am I going to maintain this perkiness for more than a few hours? During the quarantine, I had made a few attempts to push my prayer life back on track as it was beginning to sag. I'd make a good start in the beginning, only to run out of steam within the first few days and be right back at the place of deficiency and disappointment. So, the excitement of this latest round of enthusiasm was tempered with a sense of dread. Yes, that's right, this preacher who has preached the gospel for over forty years was struggling with being consistent. I have discovered that this is a struggle that never goes away, and the pandemic put my struggle in the spotlight.

I knew I needed something that would have strength built into it, something that would give me some staying power. The thought came to me, "You need to pray this prayer every hour on the hour." There it was, I had a plan. I went to the app store on my smartphone, downloaded an hourly chime app, and began to pray this simple prayer every hour on the hour from 6:00 a.m. to 11:00 p.m.

At this point, there was no story. This little practice was pulling me back into the regimen that had blessed my life for so long. I was slowly but surely beginning to get back to a consistent prayer life. Hooray for me! End of story.

But God intended to use this little practice for broader and higher purposes. Here's how He opened my eyes to that.

A few days after my shower epiphany, after I had downloaded the chime app and had begun praying every hour, I was taking Katie (my wife of 49 years) to the doctor's office. We were having what I have referred to many times in my preaching as "intense fellowship." We were arguing. I couldn't tell you what the topic was if my life depended on it. Suffice it to say, she was getting on my nerves, and I was getting on hers. I was about to deliver a full-throated response to something she had said, which was designed to elicit this very response (just old couple stuff—nothing serious). Just as I drew in the breath to deliver my diatribe, my hourly chime sounded. I put up my index finger and said, "Hold on, I have to do this." I closed my eyes and went into the Lord's prayer with her staring at me. Luckily, we were at a stoplight.

"Why are you praying like that?" she asked.

"What?" I responded, "I can't pray?"

"You know what I mean," she said. "You broke into prayer right in the middle of our conversation."

I said, "When you come out of the doctor's office, I'll tell you the whole story." She was going in for her routine checkup. All is well with her, thank the Lord.

On the short ride back home, I explained my shower epiphany to her and how I was praying every hour. "I want to pray with you," she said. So we began to pray every hour on the hour, sometimes together, sometimes in separate spaces.

At the end of the first week of us praying together, I asked Katie how this regimen was working for her.

She said, "Two things are happening. One, I feel connected to you every hour because I know whether we are in the same space or not, we are praying together. And two, praying this short prayer every hour helps me stay grounded and reminded of why we're here, to see God's kingdom come and His will done on earth."

I was feeling the same way. It was comforting to me and strengthening our relationship to know that wherever we were, at the sound of the chime, we were praying the same prayer. My focus on God and His Kingdom had never been this high consistently throughout the day since I started walking with God.

That's when it began to dawn on me that this little practice had larger implications than I had imagined and that God was opening a time and opportunity for the Church to shine.

Christians are feeling isolated and disconnected from their church community while pastors are grappling with how to keep the flock fed, protected, and together.

Even larger issues are looming. Our nation is experiencing a medical, financial, and social crisis that none of us have experienced in our lifetime. Yet, in the midst of this rancorous time for our nation, the Church can, by simple obedience, perform a simple act that can simultaneously draw it close to God and turn the world right-side up.

CHAPTER 2

"OUR FATHER IN HEAVEN"

OUR FATHER

What a powerful revelation these first two words convey. The first thing to notice is we are told in this prayer to use the plural possessive noun "our" when we address God instead of the singular possessive pronoun "my." Why? Is it that God is opposed to singular prayer, or is He not interested in the individual? Not at all. God is extremely interested in the individual. Classic teaching on God's extreme interest in the individual is found in the three parables in **Luke 15:** The Lost Sheep, The Lost Coin, and the Lost (Prodigal) Son. The point of these three parables is that God is very much focused on the individual. Such a comforting revelation. Jesus explained in **Matt. 10** that the Father is so focused on you that "the very hairs of your head are all numbered." God loves the individual.

The point of us addressing God as our Father collectively is to underscore the most dynamic principle of prayer: the principle of agreement. For our prayer to be effective, it must first be in accord with God's will; **1 John 5.14-15** "Now this is the confidence that we have in Him, that if we ask anything according to His will, He hears us. (15) And if we know that he hears us, whatever we ask, we know we have the petitions that we have asked of Him." (NKJV)

Being in agreement with God's will is the main thing, but it is not the only thing. The flip side of that coin is to be in agreement with God's people, your brothers and sisters. God wants you to understand that you are not alone. From the very beginning, God declared, "It is not good for man to be alone." **Gen. 2.18** (NIV)

The greatest witnesses of Christ's reality will not be miracles performed by us or the persuasiveness of the pulpit preachers. No, instead, the power of God will be manifested in our unity. Jesus put it this way in **John 17.21b**, "That they may also be one in Us, that the world may believe that You sent Me." (NKJV)

Our unity, our connection to one another in faith, which is worked out by love, will be the most tangible witness of the life, death, and resurrection of the Lord Jesus Christ.

What I am suggesting as a manifestation of this gospel truth is for the Church, The Body of Christ, to make a public display of our unity that transcends political boundaries, ethnic boundaries, socio-economic boundaries, generational boundaries, and even geographic boundaries. It's time for God the Father to be Our Father.

Jesus said in **Matt. 18.19,** "Again I say to you that if two of you agree on earth concerning anything they ask, it will be done for them by my Father in heaven." (NIV)

When the Church gets into agreement around the things we can agree on, we become the salt and light Jesus called us to be. We must not let ourselves be distracted by things that have no eternal value, like skin color or political party affiliation.

We can all agree that God is our Father and Jesus Christ is our Lord, and the Lord Jesus told us to pray together and address God collectively as OUR FATHER.

What would your city or town look like if all the people who have been washed by the blood of Jesus Christ stopped at the top of every hour and held up an index finger, as it were, to the whole world and said, "Hold on, we have to do this?" And then twenty thousand, or one hundred and fifty thousand, or one and a half million believers at the same time and in the same city said: "Our Father who is in heaven, hallowed be your name, your Kingdom come, your will be done on earth as it is in heaven…."

David the Psalmist envisioned a world where brothers, people who had the same Father, dwelt together in unity. He put it like this in **Ps. 133.1-3** "Behold how good and how pleasant it is for brethren to dwell together in unity! (2) It is like the precious oil upon the head, running down on the beard, the beard of Aaron, running down on the edge of his garments. (3) It is like the dew of Hermon, descending upon the mountains of Zion; for there the Lord commanded the blessing—Life forevermore." (NKJV)

When the people of God act like the single family that we are, when brothers from every ethnicity, every political party, every stratum of the socio-economic scale, drop all those ancillary identities and identify with Christ our Elder Brother and God our Father, God has a standing order for His blessing to show up in the place where that happens.

Before the Civil War in America, several nationwide church denominations split over the issues surrounding the war. Kentucky Senator Henry Clay called the phenomenon of the Church splits "the greatest source of danger to our country" (*Christian History* magazine #33).

As the Church goes, so goes the nation. O please, God, don't let this generation of the Church stand before you with the blood of this nation's discord on our hands— please, O Lord, let us be agents of reconciliation. Lord, let us find the grace to "Maintain the unity of the Spirit in the bond of Peace." **Eph. 4.3** (ESV)

Jesus said to us, "You are the salt of the earth, but if the salt loses its flavor, how shall it be seasoned? It is good for nothing but to be thrown out and trampled underfoot by men. You are the light of the world." **Matt. 5.13-14a** (NKJV)

Only the Church can counteract the rottenness of hatred in our culture. Only the Church can light up the path to the Shalom of God, the peace and prosperity that God desires for our world. Could it be that the path out of the sickness and darkness of the pandemic will be lit and led by the Church? And could it be that the first step for the church is to get herself in sync by the profoundly simple act of praying city-wide, nationwide, worldwide together every hour?

May this generation of the Church bring preservation and illumination to a world going rotten in the darkness of hopelessness and hatred.

CHAPTER 3

"YOUR KINGDOM COME, YOUR WILL BE DONE ON EARTH AS IT IS IN HEAVEN"

Something special happens when the people of God get in sync with each other. Let's look at the birth of the Church. **Acts 2.1** says, "When the day of Pentecost had fully come, they were all with one accord in one place." (NKJV) The world is still reeling from what happened next in that place, and it is still going on. The Church was born. On that day of Pentecost, this ragtag group of followers of the Carpenter from Galilee became the first members of the Body of Christ.

The journey to this place of "one accord" was not easy. These disciples didn't wake up that morning and say while they were doing their morning stretch, "Hmm, think I'll pop over to the prayer meeting in the upper room." No, these one hundred and twenty disciples had slogged for the better part of three years around the land of Palestine with The Teacher, in and out of synagogues and the temple, humble homes, and palatial dwellings of the rich and famous of Israel. There was the constant pressure of adoring crowds and groupies, as well as murderous plots. Then came the raid in the Garden of Gethsemane. Jesus was seized, and Peter succumbed to the pressure of the moment and took to violence. Later, he denied he even knew Jesus. Then the trial and the crucifixion and the mocking and jeering from the crowds and then—He was dead! Jesus, the hope of all His disciples, was dead, hanging from the cross, then buried in a tomb he didn't even own.

On the third day after Jesus died came the resurrection. What started as rumors early that Sunday morning culminated with the resurrected Christ walking through the locked doors where the frightened disciples had gathered.

This group of disciples had experienced the deepest of depths and the highest of highs, and everything else in between. According to **1 Cor. 15**, over five hundred people saw the resurrected Christ with their own eyes, and He told them all to wait in Jerusalem for the promise of the Father; yet, there were only one hundred and twenty of them in the upper room in Jerusalem. These people fought the "good fight of faith" to be in the upper room at this time. There was so much uncertainty, so much opportunity for anxiety. No one had a clue what was going to happen. Of all the things that could have been noted, the Holy Spirit directed our attention to the fact that "They were all with one accord." The word "accord" is from the word family we get the word "homogeneous." In modern parlance, we use the word homogeneous to signify the sameness of a group, such as the same race, same socio-economic strata, and so on. To be sure, these one hundred and twenty disciples were about as homogeneous, outwardly speaking, as a group could get. Most of them were from the same region of Galilee and Capernaum. Many of them were related to each other. They were all Jews, with the possible exception of Luke, a Greek. They were all small business owners or members of the working class. This was about as homogeneous a group as you could get. No story there. That happens every Sunday across the globe. The vast majority of church congregations that gather in the USA and across the globe are homogeneous, having similar ethnicity, similar socio-economics, and whatever else that makes them comfortable with each other.

Here's the story; in the second to the last verse of **Acts 2**, that exact word "accord" is used again to describe the state of the gathered people. Someone looking at the one hundred and twenty disciples gathered in the upper room on the morning of Pentecost Sunday might have thought that this group's homogeneity came from the fact that all the outward elements were the same. But by the end of that day, all the outward elements were drastically different. There would be absolutely no way to draw that same conclusion by looking at this group. There were dark-skinned, medium-hued, and very light-skinned individuals, with every hair texture imaginable. There were dozens of different native tongues represented in this group; every economic stratum represented from the very rich to the very poor. They were from the four corners of the earth. As about diverse a group that could be assembled, yet they were homogeneous, "in one accord."

Their homogeneity didn't come from any external cues. Their one accord came from the fact that they all shared the same source of life. It was one life in all of them, or more exactly one Spirit that was the source of life for every person added to the Church that day and every day after that day. The Holy Spirit of God had grafted them all into the True Vine, Jesus Christ, the Root of Jesse.

We don't all need to try to assemble in a multi-ethnic congregation. Quite frankly, that is not an easy feat to accomplish. The simple fact is there are not as many opportunities across this country and across the globe as one might think for a multi-ethnic, diverse socio-economic group to come together in a single congregational setting. Why? Because most congregations are situated in largely non-diverse communities, and congregations tend to reflect the demographic composition of the communities in which they are embedded.

The creative and dedicated people that give leadership and membership to multi-ethnic congregations should be commended. It is not easy work; it takes commitment and intentionality every day of its existence. That said, what I am about to say is in no way a denigration of the godly example that a multi-ethnic congregation presents to the world of the diversity of the Body of Christ globally. As beautiful and hopeful as they are, multi-ethnic congregations are not where the rubber meets the road, but the multi-ethnic church is. Let me explain.

While a multi-ethnic congregation takes spiritual maturity, creativity, and commitment to pull off, it only happens in a multi-ethnic community. I have lived and ministered in Chicago all my life. Chicago has been dubbed as the most American city in the United States, meaning Chicago reflects the American ethos of diversity and segregation to an extent not seen in many other places.

This city has also been dubbed one of the most segregated cities in America. I don't agree with that branding, but I understand how one could draw that conclusion. There are seventy-seven distinct neighborhoods in this city. Dr. John Fuder has written a book that highlights each one of the Chicago neighborhoods titled: "Chicago Neighborhood Prayer Guide: *Seeking God's Peace for the City.*" Many of these distinct neighborhoods grew around immigrant populations that poured into this city from all over the world around the turn of the last century. To give an example of how many immigrant groups make up the population of this city, Lane Technical High School on Chicago's north side was once in the Guinness World Records book for having the most nationalities represented in one school.

There are a million African Americans living on the south and west sides of the city that arrived here during the "Great Migration" of the 1940s, where millions of African Americans moved from the south to industrial cities of the north to fill the factory jobs during WWII. Chicago has a large Latin population of several hundred thousand, many of whom live in the Pilsen neighborhood.

This city has the largest Polish population outside of Poland. Chicago hosts a large Italian community centered around Taylor Street, which is appropriately called "Little Italy." There is a thriving Chinese population in Chinatown. There's the Ukrainian Village with over one hundred thousand Ukrainian ex-pats. There is a large eastern Indian population around Devon Street on the north side. There are large and proud Irish and Swedish communities that help build this city into the thriving metropolis that it is today.

However, Chicago is not a melting-pot. These groups did not melt down and become one homogeneous community. Several factors played into keeping the immigrant communities separated, such as unequal access to capital for homeownership and restrictive covenants on home sales. Those issues are explored by other books. The point here is that because of all the forces and agendas that kept the ethnic communities separated in Chicago, and for that matter, cities all across this country, America is not a melting pot, contrary to the romantic poetic notions portrayed in the past. For better or worse, that's the reality. What we are is more like a salad bowl. A salad bowl is where the tomatoes bring something different to the mix than the onion, and the croutons are encouraged to bring the crunch, while the boiled eggs are celebrated for their smoothness. In the same way, each community has its flair, which contributes to the vitality of the whole city.

There are a number of congregations that meet in Chicago that have a diverse population that represent several ethnic groups and diverse socio-economic lines. These congregations exist largely in pockets on the north side of the city, where the neighborhoods tend to be more diverse. However, these congregations represent only a small fraction of the four thousand total congregations of the city. For the most part, the Polish saints like to meet on Sunday with the other Polish saints. The congregations in the Ukrainian village like the worship services in their language. The congregations that meet in Pilsen like their Spanish language services. The congregations in the African American communities like the flow of their services, and the congregations in white communities like the flow of their worship gatherings.

There is a hopeful phenomenon we have been experiencing in Chicago over the last several years. Dr. John Fuder heads up an organization called "Chicagoland United In Prayer" (CUIP), formerly "Pray Chicago." CUIP is the daughter organization of Together Chicago, which I will talk more about later.

Every year for the last ten years, CUIP has organized a prayer gathering on the last Sunday in January for Chicagoland (city and suburbs). The last in-person gathering on Sunday, January 26, 2020, had almost 100 different congregations represented from every neighborhood and ethnic group in the city. What we have witnessed in these gatherings is nothing short of amazing — individual congregations in this city coming together and praying together as One Church in Chicago. White congregations, African American congregations, Latin congregations, Korean congregations, Chinese congregations, Eastern Indian congregations, and more, coming together and being The One Church in the city.

What our cities need, what our nation needs, is for the congregations that call on the name of Jesus Christ to be as One Body. The Apostle Paul put it this way in **Eph. 4.4,** "There is one body and one Spirit, just as you were called in one hope of your calling; (5) one Lord, one faith, one baptism; (6) one God and Father of all, who is above all, and through all, and in you all." (NKJV)

Jesus told us to pray "Our Father." He told us to pray, "Your Kingdom come, Your will be done on earth as it is in heaven."

This pandemic has restricted individual congregations from gathering in individual buildings.

Instead of allowing that to be a hindrance, I believe it has opened the door for the Church's finest hour. We get to demonstrate that we are larger than one congregation. We get to demonstrate that we cannot be contained in one building, just like our God cannot be contained in one building; instead, He has chosen to reside in the hearts of all His children.

We are the salt of the earth, we are the light of the world, and we can become one, every hour on the hour, no matter where in the world we are. What would happen if ten thousand people in one city prayed the same prayer, at the same time, several times per day? I don't know, but I sure would love to find out, wouldn't you? What if it were one hundred thousand or half a million? What if ten million believers in America prayed the prayer Jesus gave us at the same time several times per day? I think heaven would open up, and God would pour healing on our land.

CHAPTER 4

"GIVE US THIS DAY OUR DAILY BREAD"

No one alive has witnessed times more challenging than these. One would have to go to the history books to read about times that parallel our present times. These times are going to be chronicled, and future generations will read about us. No quarter of the globe will go unaffected. Some are feeling the strain more than others, and the end has not yet come. So many people are feeling the strain to their supply line, and feelings of worry rise in them.

That's why Jesus told us to pray the way He did. He understands that when we feel our needs so acutely, the tendency of our human nature is for us to start our conversation with the Lord with what we need and how we feel about it. God chose to become a man in the person of Jesus Christ so that He could feel everything we would feel and face everything we would face so that He could have compassion on us, having traveled the exact same road.

"Our Father, who is in heaven, holy is Your name"

Jesus' instruction to us is, "When you pray, do it in this manner." He tells us to first focus on the God of Heaven as our Father. Our God is the Invisible God, the God who is a Spirit, from whom comes all life, who Himself is more powerful than anything seen and unseen. He has no beginning of days nor end of time. The eternal, only Wise God has sent His Spirit to dwell in us and has given us the Spirit of Adoption, whereby we cry Abba Father. God has made us His children and, by legal action of heaven, has made us His heirs.

Then He tells us to focus our attention on the exaltation of His name, which includes His character and power. God is love—and you and I are the objects of His love; that's His character. God is almighty, He has never failed and will never fail, the only thing He cannot do is lie; that's His power. He always tells the truth, and He said, "I will never leave you or forsake you." God has not abandoned you, and even right now, despite the appearances of your circumstances, God has not forsaken you and He is making all things work together for your good.

"Your Kingdom come, Your will be done on earth as it is in heaven"

Then Jesus told us to declare God's Kingdom on the earth and petition that God's will be done on earth as it is in heaven.

THE ORDER IS IMPORTANT

This is the order in which we should make our approach to God. This order is so important because it ensures that by the time we come to mentioning our needs to God, it will be done in the context of God's greatness, power, and ability. On the other hand, if we approach God and lead with our needs first because we feel overwhelmed, we will surely be tempted to see God in the context of our need and have our hearts overtaken by fear and doubt; it's only human nature. When you come to God and lead with your need, your need fills up your line of sight, fills up your imagination, and your need seems to become larger than God.

I am telling you, as one who has been through the fire and the flood, who has experienced great heights and the deepest of depths, God your Father, Jesus Christ your Good Shepherd, and the Holy Spirit your Comforter is not going to abandon you. You are going to make it through all this and see the goodness of the Lord.

As you focus on God your Father and remind yourself how Great He is, how powerful He is, how much He loves you, that truth begins to lift you up and give you a drastically different perspective on your needs, and He begins to fill your heart and your imagination.

In 1959, when I was nine years old, my dad and my uncle took my brother and me along with them to drive from Chicago to New York City to bring Nana, my grandmother, back to live with us. While we were there in New York, we went to Ellis Island to see the Statue of Liberty. I recall the awe I felt as I stood at the base of that mighty statue and peered up at it. The largest human-like figure I had ever seen before or since. It filled my entire view. Besides meeting my grandmother for the first time, it was the highlight of the whole trip.

Fast forward forty-one years to 2010. I was flying into New York City to attend an event at the United Nations building. We landed at La Guardia Airport. Before the trip, I studied Google Maps so that I could approximately identify Ellis Island if we happened to fly by it in our approach to the airport. Sure enough, we did, and studying the map helped me identify it. There it was, Ellis Island, a small dot in the water of the Hudson River, and the noble lady on her multi-pointed base was even smaller. What a difference perspective makes. Standing at the base and looking up at that mighty statue, my entire view was filled by her presence. Quite a difference from flying by thousands of feet in the air; I had to concentrate and squint to find her.

So it is when you focus on your problems. They can overwhelm you and fill your view and imagination and overshadow and cool off your faith. But when you focus on God's love toward you and His power to make His love come to bear on you and your life, at that moment, your need becomes a speck, and God's arm is seen for what it is—Almighty. Your spirit rises into the direct light of His glory and your faith, as it were, heats up.

Instead of leading our prayer with our need, we lead our prayer by celebrating God's Fatherhood over us, the beauty and power of His name, the relentless inevitability of His Kingdom. When you approach God in that order, joy floods your heart, your faith becomes strong, and you stop worrying and start believing God and thanking Him. **Phil. 4.6-7** "Be anxious for nothing, but in everything by prayer and supplication, with thanksgiving, let your requests be made known to God; (7) and the peace of God which surpasses all understanding, will guard your hearts and minds through Christ Jesus." (NKJV)

CHAPTER 5

"FORGIVE US OUR DEBTS AS WE FORGIVE OUR DEBTORS"

The whole crux of the gospel is the forgiveness of sin. There is no way to overstate the magnitude of the forgiveness of God purchased by the blood of Jesus. So crucial is forgiveness to the gospel that Jesus said, in essence, the only proof you have of being forgiven is embedded in your forgiveness of others. He said it like this in **Matt. 6.14-15**, "For if you forgive men their trespasses, your heavenly Father will also forgive you. (15) But if you do not forgive men their trespasses, neither will your Father forgive your trespasses." (NKJV)

The lesson here is simple: no one can cover the debt owed to the holiness of God for even the smallest infraction without going into debtor's prison forever.

It's not that God is so stubborn or intolerant that the slightest infraction is such a big deal. That's not the case at all. The fact is that the glory of God's presence is so absolutely pure and holy that it would be blasphemous to allow the slightest dishonoring of that absolute glory to go unresolved. God cannot deny Himself.

But thanks be to God, who took all of this into consideration before he uttered the first word of creation. God is not a creator who had to become a redeemer when His creation, man, got himself into trouble in the Garden of Eden. No, we were chosen "in Him before the foundation of the world." **Eph. 1.4** (NKJV)

God created man such that He, Himself, would become a man in the person of His Son Jesus. Jesus, who called Himself "The Son of Man," so that He could stand in the stead of every man, absorb our offenses, and "drink the cup" of sin for all mankind, thus taking all of our offenses to the grave with Him and imparting His righteousness to us who receive it by faith. "Thanks be to God for His indescribable gift." **2 Cor. 9.15** (NKJV)

Nothing is more vital to our life than forgiveness. Forgiveness is the air we breathe. Without it, we have no relationship with God the Father. What the world needs is to be led into the place of the forgiveness of God. But so many don't even think that place exists. But we, as children of God, who call God "Our Father," know forgiveness, and the evidence of our knowledge of God's forgiveness is that we have forgiveness to give. If you cannot forgive, that is the clearest indication that you have not received your forgiveness by faith. Let's not sugar coat this critical issue—your soul salvation hangs on the ability to receive and give forgiveness. To refuse to receive or give forgiveness is to trample underfoot the Blood of Jesus, who purchased our forgiveness.

Our nation is being stressed at the seams because of intolerance and unforgiveness. The only institution in this nation, nay in the world, that can administer true forgiveness is the Church. The tension and polarization in the political arena are sharp; the tension between the various ethnic groups in this nation is sharp. The relationship between the African American community and the police is full of tension. The intolerance toward divergent political views and positions continue to drive a wedge between various communities in this country. The only balm for the self-inflicted wounds of this nation is found in the Church. Forgiveness is that balm that can soothe the wounds our world faces.

I have been preaching this glorious gospel since 1974. I have had the privilege of grooming men and women for full-time gospel ministry as well as impactful marketplace ministry. One of the questions I have trained myself and my trainees to answer when presenting gospel truth is, "What does this truth look like in practice?" The Epistle of Philemon presents a real-life illustration of *forgiveness in action*.

In this letter, the Apostle Paul writes personally to his dear friend, fellow laborer, and brother Philemon. It is clear by the content of this short letter that at some time previously, Philemon came to faith in Christ through the ministry of Paul and that Philemon, for a time, attached himself to Paul to assist him in his ministry. What developed was a deep brotherly love between these two men.

Then Paul moved on to other ministry assignments. In time, he met Onesimus and led him to faith in Christ. Onesimus joined himself to Paul and served him in the ministry. He became Paul's "son in the gospel." He was a help to Paul at a critical time in his life because Paul found himself imprisoned for preaching this gospel, and Onesimus was a lifeline for him in jail.

When Paul discovered that Onesimus was an indentured servant of Philemon and that he had run away without satisfying his debt, Paul sent Onesimus back to Philemon. He sent him with this handwritten note, which made its way into the canon of scripture.

The essence of this letter says, this man who was a useless slave to you (Onesimus roughly translates to unprofitable) has become my son. I am asking you to forgive this man his debt and put the balance he owes to you against the balance you owe to me.

In this short little handwritten note, the gospel truth of forgiveness is played out. Onesimus had breached his obligation of the debt he owed to Philemon. The society of that day was strict about fulfilling those obligations. A breach of that obligation could, in some cases, be a capital offense.

What caused him to run away from Philemon's house and put his life in jeopardy? God only knows why he did, and God also knew that in his running, Onesimus would run into Paul, and in so doing, he would run into the arms of God the Father and become one of His sons. Thanks be to God who has caused so many of us who were running away from our obligations to run into Him.

And now Onesimus was Philemon's brother. However, nothing else had changed. He still had an obligation to Philemon, he was still a runaway slave, and he still had to face the music—and face it he would. Only now he would do so with more than just a letter from Paul, as powerful as it was. Onesimus would face his brother Philemon with the same Spirit in him that was in his brother.

In our torn culture, there is a lot of offense to go around—no one, no individual, no group is innocent or without blame. There is enough blame to go around, and everyone can get a full portion. The only remedy is for us to humble ourselves before God and before each other and extend forgiveness to each other as we have received it from God our Father because the same Spirit that is giving me life is giving that same life to my brother.

No matter what our historical posture has been, today, we call on God as "Our Father." In order for this world to be healed, we, the Body of Christ, His Church, have to extend the healing grace of forgiveness to each other. We become the "binding agent" that will close the wounds of this nation.

CHAPTER 6

"DELIVER US FROM THE EVIL ONE"

T his chapter will lay bare the number one tactic of the evil one to tempt God's people away from Him and into worry and will show you how to counteract that tactic.

Gen. 3.1-6 *Now the serpent was more crafty than any other beast of the field that the LORD GOD had made.*

He said to the woman, "Did God actually say, 'You shall not eat of any tree in the garden'?" (2) And the woman said to the serpent, "We may eat of the fruit of the trees in the garden, (3) but God said, 'You shall not eat of the fruit of the tree in the midst of the garden, neither shall you touch it, lest you die.'" (4) But the serpent said to the woman, "You will surely not die. (5) For God knows that when you eat of it your eyes will be opened, and you will be like God, knowing good and evil." (6) So when the woman saw that the tree was good for food, and that it was a delight to the eyes, and that the tree was to be desired to make one wise, she took of the fruit and ate, and she also gave some to her husband who was with her, and he ate. (ESV)

Matt. 4.1-11 *Then Jesus was led up by the Spirit into the wilderness to be tempted by the devil. (2) And after fasting forty days and forty nights, he was hungry. (3) And the tempter came and said to him, "If you are the Son of God, command these stones to become loaves of bread." (4) But he answered, "It is written, 'Man shall not live by bread alone, but by every word that comes from the mouth of God.'"*

(5) Then the devil took him to the holy city and set him on the pinnacle of the temple (6) and said to him, "If you are the Son of God, throw yourself down, for it is written, "'He will command his angels concerning you,' and "'On their hands they will bear you up, lest you strike your foot against a stone.'"

(7) Jesus said to him, "Again it is written, 'You shall not put the Lord your God to the test.'" (8) Again, the devil

took him to a very mountain and him all the kingdoms of the world and their glory. (9) And said to him, "All these I will give you, if you will fall down and worship me." (10) Then Jesus said, "Be gone, Satan! For it is written, 'You shall worship the Lord your God and him only shall you serve.'"

(11) Then the devil left him, and behold, the angels came and were ministering to him. (ESV)

What kinds of conversations are you having?

When God created Adam and put him in the Garden of Eden, He gave him specific instructions not to eat the fruit from a certain tree located in the center of the garden called the "tree of the knowledge of good and evil." Then God created a woman to help him and complete him. God would visit them in the cool of the day, probably morning and evening, and would have conversations with them.

Then one day, the serpent began a conversation with the woman. (It was not until after the sin in the garden did the woman receive a name different from Adam; after the fall, she was called Eve, before that, they together were Adam).

During these conversations, the serpent convinced the woman that God was withholding something good and desirable from her and that she needed to take an action that was contrary to what God had explicitly forbidden. He tricked her with deceitful information and outright lies and got her to take harmful action against her own soul. During this fateful conversation, the serpent convinced the woman that what God was withholding was the very thing she wanted. She didn't want the tree or anything from the tree before her conversation with the serpent; only after the conversation did she seem to want the fruit. What God was withholding from this husband and wife was death, and the serpent, in a carefully crafted conversation with the woman, dislodged the truth and replaced it with a lie.

She ate the fruit from the forbidden tree, and then she gave that fruit to her husband, and he ate, so death gained a stronghold on the human race. And it all started with a conversation.

Eve had a conversation with the serpent, and it ended in not only her destruction but ours. The serpent presented thoughts and ideas in their conversation that were contrary to the Truth of God's Word. That's what he does, so I ask again, what kinds of conversations are you having?

Let's look at another conversation the serpent had. In this conversation, he is not called the serpent; he is called by his real name, Satan. We see that he uses the same tactics, but this conversation did not go in his favor. This was the conversation between Satan and Jesus after He had fasted for forty days and forty nights. It went poorly for Satan, not because Jesus exerted His Divinity against the devil. He didn't do that at all. Jesus didn't match wits with the devil—that would be no contest, and the devil would be infinitely outmatched. Instead, Jesus stayed within the parameters of His humanity and used only those weapons that He left to you and me to resist the temptations of the evil one.

After His baptism in the Jordan River by His cousin, John the Baptizer, Jesus was compelled by the Holy Spirit to go into the desert for the express purpose of being tempted by the devil. In other words, Jesus was sent to have a conversation with the devil. There is so much that can be learned from this exchange that volumes of books have been written about this confrontation. I just want to highlight one thing, probably the main takeaway from this fateful conversation with the devil.

Every idea, every proposition presented by the devil to Jesus was measured by the Word of God, and the flaws and deficiencies of the devil's thoughts and ideas were immediately made apparent and rejected.

This is not to say that the devil presents ideas that are so outlandish that we couldn't possibly conceive of accepting them; quite the contrary, the virtue of a good counterfeit is how much it looks like the real thing. The devil always speaks to the real issues of life, and unless you know and understand the Word of God, you may not spot his wicked and perverted twist on matters.

In this instance, Jesus had fasted for forty days and forty nights, and he was genuinely hungry. The devil understood that fact. He was very familiar with the human appetite and has spent long centuries tricking people into all kinds of rebellious ways to satisfy their God-given desires and appetites.

Here, Satan tries to proposition Jesus to satisfy His hunger in a way that was independent from God. "Take matters into your own hands, you don't know when God is going to let you eat something" was the essence of what the devil was suggesting to Jesus, much in the same way he had proposed to Eve. He suggested to Eve that she had to experience for herself the properties of the fruit because he had convinced her in their conversation that she couldn't take God at His Word.

Jesus' response to Satan's proposition laid out for us a principle for life. He said, "It is written," meaning the only effective response to Satan's onslaught is the Word of God. Jesus Christ, who calls Himself in Revelation "The First and the Last; The Beginning and the End," is the prevailing Truth against any and every lie of the devil. Jesus said, "I Am the Truth." The only way to answer the temptation of the evil one is by the Word of God Himself. Jesus showed us that instead of trying to match wits with the devil, we should rely on the Word of God to answer the devil's propositions and guide our actions.

The answer Jesus gave is from **Deut. 8.3**, "Man... lives...by the Word of God."

He affirmed that it is not physical sustenance or the food in our bellies that keeps us alive; after all, there are people who have died on a full stomach. What keeps us alive is what God has declared about us and our lives. We need food and water and shelter and clothing, but those things in and of themselves don't keep us alive. Jesus demonstrated by this forty-day fast during which His life was held intact by God's declaration about Him. You and I have a life that is not as dependent on the physical amenities that sometimes drive us into panic mode.

In the second temptation, Satan pivoted and used or misused the scriptures. He quotes **Ps. 91.11-12**, but he gives a bogus application. The whole theme of **Ps. 91** is intimacy with God. It talks about the secret place of the Most High God, and it uses the metaphor of being covered by God's feathers, reminiscent of the way a mother eagle covers her eggs. You can't get much closer than that. Out of that intimacy comes this unconditional trust in the protection of God. **Ps. 91.8** says, "Only with your eyes shall you look, and see the reward of the wicked." (NKJV)

This is the trust the Father was looking for from Adam in the garden, standing there in front of the tree of the knowledge of good and evil. He didn't want them to experience the evil of that fruit. He wanted them to trust Him, take His absolutely reliable word for it, and know just by looking at it that it would kill them because He said it would. Satan convinced them to put God to the test, "will it really kill you?" he asked. The answer was yes, it would and did kill them and every child born from them.

Again, Jesus responded from the Word, "It is written, 'You shall not put the Lord you God to the test.'" **Num. 23.19** puts it like this "God is not a man, that He should lie, or a son of a man that He should change his mind. Has He said, and will He not do it? Or has He spoken, and will He not fulfill it?" (ESV)

The third temptation was brazen on its face. It laid bare the myopic view of Satan compared to the eternal, everlasting view of the King of Kings and the Lord of Lords, who will reign in a new heaven and a new earth forever and ever in the ages to come. Satan was offering

Jesus this world, which is slated for destruction, and everything in it, all of which is fodder for the flames, in exchange for Jesus abdicating his eternal glorious throne.

That deal is like the devil standing in front of an ice cream factory, holding an ice cream bar made in the factory with some melted ice cream in it that he picked out of the trash and offering it to Jesus in exchange for the keys and ownership of the factory.

I have heard of bad deals, but no deal can be concocted in the history of all deals that could come close to being as bad as this deal that Satan was offering to Jesus. When you think of it, this extremely lopsided exchange Satan was offering to Jesus is not much different than the extremely lopsided temptations Satan offers to you and me. At first blush, you might ask how Satan could, with a straight face, offer such an insanely lopsided, totally bad deal to Jesus. Here's how: Satan was banking on the possibility that perhaps Jesus didn't see Himself accurately and didn't fully understand who He was. This tactic is the age-old trap the devil has laid for God's people since his encounter with the woman in the garden of Eden up until today. According to scripture, when we don't see ourselves accurately and adequately, we greatly underestimate our value and sell ourselves criminally short.

We are living in a time that none of us have ever experienced before. We live in a world where an astronomical amount of information is swirling around, and so much of it is unreliable. It is too easy to engage in "conversations" on different platforms with people who have wicked intentions or have been pushed into an angry, frightened worldview. It is way too easy to forget who you are and to whom you belong. Being reminded at the top of each hour by praying this awesome prayer, given to us by Jesus Himself, will help keep you grounded in your faith, centered on God's kingdom, and connected to your family, the Church.

PART TWO

STRATEGICALLY PRAYING THE PRAYER

CHAPTER 7

PERSONAL BENEFIT

This chapter will show you how to get the most benefit in your personal walk with God.

As mentioned earlier, I prayed the Lord's prayer while in a dry place, feeling unmotivated and disconnected from God. It had been a while since I had felt connected to Him and motivated and hopeful about the future. But the cumulative effect of that one prayer was that I got a sense that this would be a turning point, so I committed to praying this prayer at the beginning of every hour during the day. After downloading a ninety-nine-cent mobile app and setting it to chime every hour between 6:00 a.m. and 11:00 p.m., I began to pray the Lord's Prayer every hour. At the very first hour, the clouds did not clear, the birds did not begin to chirp, nor did a bright ray of sunshine hit my face. It didn't happen that way. The first couple of days were novel and encouraging because it was a plan.

There is almost no stopping a person who has a plan. A plan helps you keep taking forward steps. A plan answers the question, "What do I do next?" The beauty of this plan was its sheer simplicity. I didn't have to figure out anything else except respond when the phone chimed by closing my eyes, folding my hands, and speaking to God my Father with the words that Jesus explicitly told me to pray. Jesus said, "When you pray, say these words…."

After the novelty wore off, the chime began to feel like an interruption. It would interrupt what would have become a Facebook binge, a melancholy pity party, or any number of unproductive tirades in which I found myself engaged. I am way old school, long before ADD was ever diagnosed, but I'm pretty sure that if I was measured by that metric, I would be diagnosed with at least a mild case. But every hour, the chime would remind me to pray, which would recenter me and get me refocused on the task at hand. In short, I became so much more productive.

At other times, the chime would feel like an affirmation break, which reminded me in the middle of my work who I belonged to and to reflect on why I was doing whatever I was doing. I became so much more enthusiastic about my work. That hourly prayer break reminded me that I am a child of God on assignment for His Kingdom. Every hour I would declare, "Your kingdom come, Your will be done on earth as it is in heaven."

After a few weeks, I was in a brand-new place spiritually. I was getting back to the regimen of prayer, Bible study, and physical exercise that was such a blessing to my life and made me so joyful and productive. My fellowship with God was beginning to be more intimate and more focused because it was all around His goodness and His kindness and His Kingdom and His will.

It was during this time that the Lord inspired/instructed me to write this little book because He wants to draw His children close to Him like this. He knows that so many of us want to have intimate fellowship with Him, but we are not sure how to do it.

Deep down inside, we know that it takes time and persistence to build an intimate and strong relationship with the Father through His Spirit. And we know that a powerful and consistent prayer life is the bedrock for such an intimate relationship, but try as we might, we have been so very inconsistent in our prayer life. I have been a pastor for forty-plus years, and it has been a constant battle to keep my prayer life fresh and vibrant. The thing that kept me vigilant in the discipline of prayer and Bible study was that I had to preach every Sunday. But after I turned over the preaching assignment to the young man that I had groomed for the position, the requirement to preach every Sunday was not there. Then the pandemic hit, and the isolation of being quarantined became a reality, and ever so gradually, I got soft in the middle spiritually. I began to look for another way to revive my prayer life and keep it fresh. The lifesaver for me was this new regimen of praying every hour. The simplicity and completeness of the Lord's prayer prayed several times per day has worked wonders to strengthen my prayer life and my faith. Please allow me to recommend this regimen as a basic building block for your personal walk with God. This little exercise, along with the Post Pandemic Prayer app, will not replace regular Bible reading and prayer, but it will provide Godly interruptions and holy reminders of whose kingdom you belong to and what your mission here really is. Along with that is an even farther-reaching reality and that is, every time the mobile app chimes, you will be joined in the same prayer by believers just like you all over your city, all over your state, all across this nation. When you pray, "Our Father…," millions of believers will be saying the same thing at the same time.

CHAPTER 8

START A MOVEMENT OF HEALING FOR THE NATION

The United States of America is beginning to emerge from very trying and testing times. Yet, as a nation, we are becoming more and more fragmented from each other. The gap between the rich and the poor has gotten wider. The gap between Republicans and Democrats has gotten deeper and intractable. The gaps between ethnic groups have become sharper and more polarized. Mistrust of the government is universal; it is within every community. The violence in the cities across our nation has taken an ungodly turn.

Our country is weaker morally and spiritually than I have ever seen it in all my seventy years. We need God's help to get through this difficult time.

There is only one institution with active branches and stations in every community in this nation. It cuts across racial lines, language lines, economic lines, political party lines, generational lines, and geographic lines. It is the only institution in all of society that is filled with people of goodwill who are connected to each other in a supernatural way.

There is a passage in scripture that has been quoted many times in many circles, but I believe that today, the time has come to apply the truth of that passage. **2 Chron. 7.14** "If My people who are called by My name humble themselves, and pray and seek My face, and turn from their wicked ways, then will I hear from heaven, and forgive their sin and heal their land." (ESV)

The wicked ways the people of God need to repent from are allowing temporal politics and racial identity to divide us. Our unity as part of the Body of Christ is far greater than any political party affiliation that this world has to offer. You and I have been grafted into the True Vine, and we are inheritors of the Kingdom of God. We, the Church, must repent from the bickering among ourselves and become the ministers of reconciliation that **2 Cor. 5.18-19** tells us we are. We have a connection to each other that transcends race, political party, economics, even geography. We are One Body, His Body.

If we, who have been purchased by the precious blood of The Lamb, allow our skin color or our political party affiliation to separate us, and if we despise the Spirit of Adoption, the Holy Spirit Himself, who makes us one family with God as our Father, then our nation will fall into vicious infighting and that blood will be on our hands when we stand before the judgment seat of Christ.

Convening a meeting where all competing factions come together and sit at a table and calmly discuss our differences until we find common ground is a bridge too far; I totally get that. Something like that is just too far beyond the realm of possibility in the present political and cultural climate in which we find ourselves today. I also think there is not enough will or relational currency within denominational church leadership to traverse the minefield of offense and grievance that exists within our nation. I don't think there is a human power that can mend the rift that is opening in this country.

These times of tension and despair are far beyond the capability of any man-made institution to bring remedy and healing. The entire world is being worn down by pandemic, economic, and racial tension. Governments are coming to the end of their ability to lead and keep the peace. If we don't see a miracle from heaven, our future is in peril.

We can pause what we are doing, for one moment on the hour, and lift our voice as the blood-bought saints of the Most High God, and call on Him in unity and say, "YOUR KINGDOM COME, YOUR WILL BE DONE ON EARTH AS IT IS IN HEAVEN."

If there ever was a time our nation needed the Church to be the Church, it is now.

Look at the explicit command from the Lord Jesus in **Luke 11.2-4**. Look at every single pronoun; they are plural possessive, "**Our** Father;" "Give **us our** daily bread;" "Forgive **us our** sins;" "For **we** also forgive everyone who is indebted to **us**;" "Do not lead **us** into temptation;" "Deliver **us** from the evil one." There is absolutely no getting around the fact that God explicitly intended for us to pray this prayer TOGETHER. There is not one singular possessive pronoun in this entire prayer that Jesus told us to pray verbatim. I believe this prayer was given to us for this day that we're in right now.

Here's the dynamic part about praying this prayer every hour: it is scripture. These are the words that came from the mouth of Jesus. The prophet Isaiah tells us: "For as the rain comes down, and the snow from heaven, and do not return there but water the earth, and make it bring forth and bud, that it may give seed to the sower and bread to the eater, So shall My Word that goes forth from

My mouth; It shall not return to Me void, but it shall accomplish what I please, and it shall prosper in the thing for which I sent it." **Isa. 55.10-11** (NKJV). As God's Word is declared, for His Kingdom to come, His will to be done in earth as it is in heaven, by thousands, by millions at the same time, that unity will have a powerful impact.

I believe these difficult times present the perfect stage for the Church embedded in each nation to begin to shine as a beacon of light. This can become the Church's finest hour to bring glory to the name of Jesus Christ.

I am not suggesting that anyone drops their political affiliation. The United States of America has thrived on a two-party system, and we need the tension of two parties to allow our democratic republic to continue to progress. And I believe Christians make excellent public servants. I am simply suggesting that we each fly the flag of Christ and make our allegiance to Him and His Kingdom rule in our hearts. Before we are anything else, we are Christ-followers, seeking to manifest and demonstrate His Kingdom in our personal and public life.

ABOUT
BISHOP EDWARD PEECHER

Chicago native. Husband and father. Revolutionary. After years of leading Chicago Embassy Church, which he founded, in 2017, Ed became the Chief Church Liaison Officer for the non-profit, collective impact organization called Together Chicago www.togetherchicago.com.

As a child of the 1960s Civil Rights movement, Ed has been involved in community engagement for nearly fifty years. He was employed by AT&T in 1969 and served the organization for many years. While at AT&T, Ed started a Bible study in its downtown headquarters after receiving the calling from Jesus Christ. In 1983, New Heritage Christian Center was formed, and two years later, Ed resigned from his Account Executive position to pastor full-time.

Ed holds a Certificate in Pastoral Studies from Moody Bible Institute (1975). He continues to guest-teach and preach at several Bible colleges and seminaries and churches. He has groomed several spiritual leaders, many of whom are serving as senior pastors locally and internationally.

Ed and his wife Katie, have three children, two of whom have preceded them into eternity. Ed and Katie celebrated their 50th Wedding Anniversary in January 2022.

Get The Post Pandemic Prayer Guide app and expand your prayer life.

Scan the QR code below to get access:

Made in the USA
Monee, IL
05 March 2023

29060648R20046